www.booksbyboxer.com

Bee Three Publishing is an imprint of Books By Boxer
Published by
Books By Boxer, Leeds, LS13 4BS, UK
Books by Boxer (EU), Dublin, D02 P593, IRELAND
Boxer Gifts LLC, 955 Sawtooth Oak Cir, VA 22802, USA

MADE IN CHINA

ISBN: 9781915410559

This book is produced from responsibly sourced paper to ensure forest management

HERE IS A QUICK GUIDE TO SOME MAIN TERMS AND GLASSES USED IN COCKTAIL MAKING.

PINT
GLASS

CHAMPAGNE
FLUTE

MARTINI
GLASS

HIGHBALL
GLASS

ROCKS
GLASS

MUDDLE

USING A BLUNT IMPLEMENT TO CRUSH AND
INFUSE LIQUIDS WITH DRY INGREDIENTS

DRY SHAKE

SHAKING THE INGREDIENTS IN A SHAKER
WITHOUT ICE

CHURN

VIGOROUSLY STIR

SHAKE

ADDING ICE AND YOUR INGREDIENTS IN A
COCKTAIL SHAKER AND SHAKING TO COOL AND
COMBINE THE DRINK

STRAIN

USED TO REMOVE ANY LARGE PULP OR EXCESS
ICE WHEN POURING

BUILD

WHEN INGREDIENTS ARE ADDED DIRECTLY INTO
THE SERVING GLASS

BEER MARGARITA

PREP TIME: UNDER 5 MINUTES

BEER AND TEQUILA... SOUNDS GROSS, RIGHT? WRONG - IT IS THE PERFECT COCKTAIL FOR A MAN WHO CAN'T MAKE HIS MIND UP!

COMPLEXITY

2

LEVEL

INGREDIENTS

* 250ML | 8.5 OZ. LAGER BEER
* 50ML | 2 OZ. TEQUILA BLANCO
* 50ML | 2 OZ. TRIPLE SEC
* 100ML | 3.5 OZ. LIME JUICE
* 1 TBSP. SIMPLE SYRUP
* ICE CUBES

METHOD

1 RUB A LIME SLICE AROUND THE RIM OF YOUR GLASS, AND RUB THE RIM IN FLAKY SEA SALT TO CREATE A SALT RIM.

2 POUR ICE INTO YOUR GLASS, AND ADD THE TEQUILA, TRIPLE SEC, LIME JUICE, AND SIMPLE SYRUP. STIR WELL.

3 FILL THE GLASS WITH YOUR BEER AND GARNISH WITH FRESH LIME.

LAGER AND LIME

PREP TIME: UNDER 1 MINUTE

A LIGHT AND ZESTY DRINK, PERFECT FOR ENJOYING IN THE SUMMER MONTHS.

COMPLEXITY LEVEL 1

INGREDIENTS

* 50ML | 2 OZ. LIME JUICE
  (OR LIME CORDIAL)
* 300ML | 12 OZ. CHILLED LAGER BEER
* LIME WEDGE TO GARNISH

METHOD

1 CHILL YOUR BEER GLASS AND ADD YOUR LIME JUICE.

2 SLOWLY POUR IN YOUR BEER OF CHOICE - THIS COULD BE A LAGER OR IPA.

3 GARNISH WITH A LIME WEDGE AND ENJOY!

SHANDY

PREP TIME: UNDER 1 MINUTE

A LIGHTER BEER OPTION PERFECT FOR A SUMMER'S DAY - NO ONE WILL EVEN KNOW IT HAS LEMON SODA IN!

COMPLEXITY LEVEL 1

INGREDIENTS

* 250ML | 8.5 OZ. LAGER BEER
* 250ML | 8.5 OZ. LEMON SODA

METHOD

1 IN A BEER GLASS, POUR YOUR LEMON SODA. SLOWLY ADD YOUR BEER AND ENJOY!

TOP TIP: IF YOU PREFER MORE BEER, YOU CAN MAKE SOMETHING CALLED A LAGER 'TOP', WHICH HAS AROUND 3/4 BEER AND 1/4 LEMON SODA.

JÄGERBOMB

PREP TIME: UNDER 2 MINUTES

THE OPPOSITE OF A FANCY SHOT, THIS IS HERBAL, STRONG, AND FULL OF ENERGY!

COMPLEXITY
2
LEVEL

INGREDIENTS

- ★ 25ML | 1 OZ. JÄGERMEISTER
- ★ 100ML | 3.5 OZ. RED BULL

METHOD

1 FILL A SHOT GLASS WITH JÄGERMEISTER AND PLACE INTO THE BOTTOM OF A ROCKS GLASS.

2 POUR YOUR RED BULL AROUND THE OUTER EDGE OF THE SHOT GLASS , SO IT DOESN'T MIX WITH THE JÄGERMEISTER. FILL TO THE TOP OF THE SHOT GLASS AND ENJOY!

BLACK AND TAN

PREP TIME: UNDER 1 MINUTE

CAN'T DECIDE BETWEEN ALE AND STOUT? WHY NOT HAVE BOTH WITH THIS LAYERED DRINK?

COMPLEXITY

2

LEVEL

INGREDIENTS

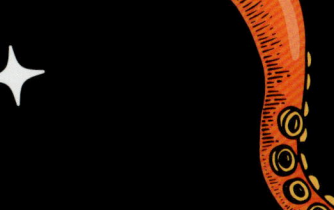

* 1/2 PINT | 8 OZ. PALE ALE
* 1/2 PINT | 8 OZ. STOUT BEER
  (E.G. GUINNESS)

METHOD

1 POUR YOUR PALE ALE INTO THE BOTTOM OF A PINT GLASS, FILLING HALFWAY.

2 ADD YOUR STOUT OVER THE ALE SLOWLY, POURING OVER THE BACK OF A TABLESPOON TO ENSURE THE LAYERS DON'T MIX!

BLACK VELVET

PREP TIME: UNDER 2 MINUTES

CHAMPAGNE? A MAN'S DRINK? WITH SOME STOUT ADDED... DEFINITELY!

COMPLEXITY
2
LEVEL

INGREDIENTS

* 50ML | 1.5 OZ. STOUT BEER (E.G. GUINNESS)
* 50ML | 1.5 OZ. CHAMPAGNE

METHOD

1 FILL YOUR CHAMPAGNE FLUTE HALFWAY WITH YOUR CHAMPAGNE.

2 POUR THE STOUT OVER THE BACK OF A TEASPOON ON TOP OF YOUR CHAMPAGNE TO CREATE LAYERS.

OLD FASHIONED

PREP TIME: UNDER 5 MINUTES

CLASSIC AND CLASSY, NOTHING SAYS 'ESTEEMED GENTLEMAN' LIKE THIS WHIKSEY SIPPER!

COMPLEXITY LEVEL 3

INGREDIENTS

* 60ML | 2 OZ. BOURBON OR WHISKEY
* 1 SUGAR CUBE
* 2-3 DASHES ANGOSTURA BITTERS
* ORANGE PEEL TWIST
* ICE CUBES

METHOD

1 IN A ROCKS GLASS, PLACE YOUR SUGAR CUBE IN THE BASE.

2 POUR YOUR BITTERS OVER THE SUGAR CUBE AND GENTLY MUDDLE TO DISSOLVE.

3 ADD A SPLASH OF WATER TO HELP FURTHER DISSOLVE THE SUGAR IF NEEDED.

4 ADD THE BOURBON OR WHISKEY TO THE GLASS.

5 FILL THE GLASS WITH ICE AND STIR GENTLY.

6 TWIST YOUR ORANGE PEEL OVER THE DRINK TO RELEASE THE OILS, THEN DROP IT INTO THE GLASS.

WHISKEY SOUR

PREP TIME: UNDER 5 MINUTES

CLASS IN A GLASS, THIS SMOKY AND SOUR DRINK IS THE PERFECT SIP FOR A MAN WANTING A REFINED DRINK THAT PACKS A PUNCH.

COMPLEXITY LEVEL 4

INGREDIENTS

- ⭐ 50ML \ 2 OZ. WHISKEY
- ⭐ 25 ML \ 1 OZ. LEMON JUICE
- ⭐ 15 ML \ 1/2 OZ. SIMPLE SYRUP
- ⭐ 1/2 FRESH EGG WHITE
- ⭐ ICE CUBES

METHOD

1 ADD THE WHISKEY, LEMON JUICE, SIMPLE SYRUP, AND EGG WHITE INTO A COCKTAIL SHAKER.

2 DRY SHAKE FOR 20 SECONDS TO LIGHTLY WHIP THE EGG WHITE.

3 ADD YOUR ICE, AND SHAKE FOR A FURTHER 15-20 SECONDS, OR UNTIL THE SHAKER IS ICE COLD TO TOUCH.

4 POUR INTO A ROCKS GLASS AND ENJOY!

THE IMPORTANCE OF ICE

ICE CAN MAKE OR BREAK YOUR COCKTAIL. EVERYONE LIKES A COLD DRINK, BUT IT'S IMPORTANT TO KNOW WHEN TO SERVE WITH ICE, OR NOT, AND EVEN WHAT TYPE OF ICE TO USE.

ON THE WHOLE, IF YOUR RECIPE CALLS FOR ICE IN STRONG AND COMPLEX DRINKS FEATURING WHISKEY OR THE LIKE, YOU'LL WANT TO USE LARGE, DRY CUBES. DRY CUBES ARE ONES THAT HAVE BEEN TAKEN STRAIGHT FROM THE FREEZER AND HAVE AN ALMOST STICKY FEEL. THESE WILL MELT SLOWLY COMPARED TO SMALLER OR SHARD-LIKE FLAKES OF ICE, WHICH WILL QUICKLY MELT AND DILUTE YOUR DRINK.

CRUSHED ICE

CRUSHED ICE IS GREAT FOR DRINKS LIKE MOJITOS, WHICH ARE ON THE SWEETER AND FRUITIER SIDE. IT ADDS TEXTURE TO THE DRINK, WHILST KEEPING IT SUPER-REFRESHING, AND ALSO DILUTES IT JUST ENOUGH SO THE SPIRITS AREN'T OVERBEARING. TO ACHIEVE CRUSHED ICE AT HOME, SIMPLY PUT ICE CUBES IN A BLENDER - JUST ENSURE THAT YOU DON'T BLEND FOR SO LONG THAT THE HEAT FROM THE BLADES MELTS ALL YOUR ICE!

LEAVE THE ICE

IF A RECIPE SAYS TO SERVE WITHOUT ICE, TRUST IT! MANY COCKTAILS WITH A LARGE SPIRIT QUANTITY AND A STRONGER FLAVOR ARE DESIGNED TO BE SIPPED AND ENJOYED LEISURELY. IF YOU ADD ICE TO THESE SORTS OF DRINKS, THE ICE WILL DILUTE YOUR DRINK OVER TIME AND YOU'LL BE LEFT WITH A COCKTAIL COMPLETELY DIFFERENT FROM THE ONE YOU STARTED WITH. REALLY WANT TO KEEP YOUR DRINK COLD? PROPERLY CHILL THE GLASS BEFOREHAND, OR INVEST IN SOME STEEL ICE CUBES – WHICH UNSURPRISINGLY, NEVER MELT!

BLOODY MARY

PREP TIME: UNDER 5 MINUTES

THE PERFECT BREAKFAST DRINK - SPICY, SAVORY, AND DELICIOUS... THERE IS NOTHING GIRLY ABOUT THIS DRINK WITH A KICK!

COMPLEXITY LEVEL 4

INGREDIENTS

- 150ML | 5 OZ. TOMATO JUICE
- 50ML | 2 OZ. VODKA
- 2 TBSP. PICKLE JUICE OR OLIVE BRINE
- 15ML | 1/2 OZ. LEMON JUICE
- 1/2 TSP. HORSERADISH
- 1/2 TSP. HOT SAUCE
- 1/2 TSP. WORCESTERSHIRE SAUCE
- CELERY TO GARNISH
- SALT AND PEPPER TO TASTE

METHOD

1 IN A MIXING GLASS, COMBINE ALL INGREDIENTS. STIR WELL.

2 ADD ICE AND SLOWLY STIR UNTIL CHILLED. TRANSFER TO A GLASS.

3 GARNISH WITH YOUR CELERY STICK AND ENJOY.

GODFATHER

PREP TIME: UNDER 2 MINUTES

SWEET, SMOKY, RICH, AND BALANCED,
NOTHING SAYS 'MACHO MAN' LIKE THE
GODFATHER.

COMPLEXITY
4
LEVEL

INGREDIENTS

* 50ML | 2 OZ. WHISKEY
* 25ML | 1 OZ. AMARETTO
* ICE CUBES

METHOD

1 FILL A COCKTAIL SHAKER WITH ICE.

2 ADD YOUR WHISKEY AND AMARETTO INTO THE SHAKER.

3 STIR WELL FOR 20-30 SECONDS UNTIL THE MIXTURE IS CHILLED.

4 STRAIN THE MIXTURE INTO A ROCKS GLASS AND ENJOY!

NEGRONI

PREP TIME: UNDER 5 MINUTES

BOLD AND TIMELESS, YOU CAN LIVE YOUR ITALIAN MOB FANTASY WITH THIS GLASS OF ITALIAN SOPHISTICATION.

COMPLEXITY
4
LEVEL

INGREDIENTS

* 25ML \ 1 OZ. GIN
* 25ML \ 1 OZ. SWEET VERMOUTH
* 25 ML \ 1 OZ. CAMPARI
* ORANGE TWIST
* ICE CUBES

METHOD

1 FILL A COCKTAIL SHAKER WITH ICE.

2 ADD YOUR WHISKEY AND AMARETTO INTO THE SHAKER.

3 STIR WELL FOR 20-30 SECONDS UNTIL THE MIXTURE IS CHILLED.

4 STRAIN THE MIXTURE INTO A ROCKS GLASS AND ENJOY!

BLACK RUSSIAN

PREP TIME: UNDER 2 MINUTES

DARK AND MYSTERIOUS, THIS COCKTAIL
WILL MAKE YOU DIM THE LIGHTS AND
GET DRINKING!

COMPLEXITY
2
LEVEL

INGREDIENTS

* 50ML | 2 OZ. VODKA
* 25ML | 1 OZ. COFFEE LIQUEUR
* ICE CUBES

METHOD

1 FILL A ROCKS GLASS WITH ICE.

2 ADD YOUR VODKA AND COFFEE LIQUEUR INTO THE GLASS.

3 STIR GENTLY TO COMBINE THE INGREDIENTS AND ENJOY!

DARK AND STORMY

PREP TIME: UNDER 2 MINUTES

STRONG AND SPICY, THIS GINGER COCKTAIL IS A GREAT VACATION DRINK THAT PACKS A PUNCH!

COMPLEXITY
2
LEVEL

INGREDIENTS

- 60ML | 2 OZ. DARK RUM
- 120ML | 4 OZ. GINGER BEER
- 15ML | 1/2 OZ. LIME JUICE
- LIME WEDGE
- ICE CUBES

METHOD

1 FILL A HIGHBALL GLASS WITH ICE.

2 POUR THE RUM AND LIME JUICE INTO THE GLASS AND STIR.

3 TOP THE DRINK WITH GINGER BEER AND STIR GENTLY.

4 GARNISH WITH A LIME WEDGE AND ENJOY!

TOP TIP: MAKE SURE YOU USE GINGER BEER AND NOT GINGER ALE IF YOU WANT THE SIGNATURE SPICY KICK.

RUM AND COKE

PREP TIME: UNDER 1 MINUTE

A CLASSIC COMBO FOR RUM LOVERS!

COMPLEXITY LEVEL 1

INGREDIENTS

- 50ML | 2 OZ. RUM
- 150ML | 5 OZ. COLA
- ICE CUBES
- LIME WEDGE

METHOD

1 FILL A ROCKS GLASS WITH ICE.

2 POUR IN YOUR RUM AND STIR TO CHILL.

3 FILL THE GLASS WITH COLA AND GARNISH WITH LIME.

TOP FOR A SWEET AND SMOKY FLAVOR, USE DARK RUM.
TIP: FOR A LIGHT AND SWEET FLAVOR, USE WHITE RUM.

DIRTY MARTINI

PREP TIME: UNDER 5 MINUTES

THIS SAVORY SIPPER WILL HAVE ALL EYES ON YOU AS THE HEIGHT OF SOPHISTICATION.

COMPLEXITY **1** LEVEL

INGREDIENTS

* 60ML | 2 OZ. GIN (OR VODKA)
* 15ML | 1/2 OZ. DRY VERMOUTH
* 15ML | 1/2 OZ. OLIVE BRINE
* GREEN OLIVES
* ICE CUBES

METHOD

1 FILL A COCKTAIL SHAKER WITH ICE.

2 POUR THE GIN (OR VODKA), DRY VERMOUTH, AND OLIVE BRINE INTO THE SHAKER.

3 STIR THE INGREDIENTS WELL FOR 20-30 SECONDS TO CHILL THE MIXTURE.

4 STRAIN THE MIXTURE INTO A CHILLED MARTINI GLASS.

5 GARNISH WITH OLIVES ON A COCKTAIL SKEWER AND ENJOY!

RUSTY NAIL

PREP TIME: UNDER 2 MINUTES

WITH A NAME LIKE 'RUSTY NAIL', NO ONE
CAN CALL THIS A GIRLY DRINK!

COMPLEXITY
1
LEVEL

INGREDIENTS

- 60ML \ 2 OZ. SCOTCH WHISKY
- 30ML \ 1 OZ. DRAMBUIE
- 1 LEMON WEDGE
- ICE CUBES

METHOD

1 FILL A COCKTAIL SHAKER WITH ICE.

2 POUR THE WHISKY AND DRAMBUIE INTO THE MIXING GLASS.

3 STIR THE INGREDIENTS WELL FOR 20-30 SECONDS TO CHILL THE MIXTURE.

4 STRAIN INTO A CHILLED ROCKS GLASS FILLED WITH ICE CUBES.

5 GARNISH WITH A LEMON WEDGE AND ENJOY!

BUT WHAT ARE BITTERS?

NO COCKTAIL MAKING CART IS COMPLETE WITHOUT SOME FORM OF BITTERS.

SO, WHAT ARE BITTERS?

ONCE USED AS MEDICINAL TONIC, THESE DAYS THEY'RE MORE COMMONLY USED AS COCKTAIL ADDITIVES. THEY'RE TYPICALLY MADE WITH HERBS, SPICES, AND BARKS, PROVIDING THEIR DISTINCTIVE FLAVOR, AND ALCOHOL.

WHAT TYPE OF BITTERS SHOULD YOU HAVE?

BEGINNERS WILL USUALLY BE FINE WITH AROMATIC BITTERS SUCH AS ANGOSTURA. THEY'RE PRETTY MUCH A STAPLE AND APPEAR IN LOTS OF CLASSIC RECIPES. BUT IF YOU WANT TO BRANCH OUT, HERE ARE SOME FLAVOR COMBINATIONS TO CONSIDER:

* AROMATIC BITTERS SUCH AS ANGOSTURA WITH OAK-AGED LIQUOR, SUCH AS WHISKEY OR BOURBON.
* CITRUS BITTERS IN COCKTAILS WITH LIGHT LIQUOR, SUCH AS VODKA OR GIN.
* PEYCHAUD'S BITTERS ARE PERFECT FOR SAZERACS – THEY BOTH ORIGINATED IN NEW ORLEANS!
* CELERY BITTERS GO WITH VERMOUTH OR SHERRY COCKTAILS, OR SAVORY COCKTAILS LIKE BLOODY MARYS.

POTABLE OR NON-POTABLE?

POTABLE - SAFE TO BE CONSUMED ON THEIR OWN, SUCH AS VERMOUTH OR CAMPARI.

NON-POTABLE - THEY'RE TOO STRONG TO BE CONSUMED ALONE, SUCH AS ANGOSTURA OR FRUIT BITTERS.

TOP TIP: IF THE RECIPE DOESN'T SPECIFY WHICH TO USE, YOUR SAFEST BET IS NON-POTABLE.

BOILERMAKER

PREP TIME: UNDER 2 MINUTES

AH YES... A MAN'S TWO FAVORITE THINGS!
BEER... AND WHISKEY... NEXT TO EACH
OTHER.

COMPLEXITY
1
LEVEL

INGREDIENTS

- ★ 1 PINT BEER
- ★ 25ML \ 1 OZ. WHISKEY

METHOD

1 POUR THE BEER INTO A PINT GLASS.

2 POUR THE WHISKEY INTO A SEPARATE SHOT GLASS.

3 SERVE SIDE BY SIDE. YES - IT'S THAT SIMPLE!

TOP TIP: TO ENJOY, TAKE A SIP OF BEER FOLLOWED BY A SIP OF WHISKEY.

SUFFERING BASTARD

PREP TIME: UNDER 3 MINUTES

TOO MANY OF THESE, AND YOU'LL BE JUST AS THE TITLE SUGGESTS!

COMPLEXITY

3

LEVEL

INGREDIENTS

- ★ 45ML | 1 1/2 OZ. GIN
- ★ 30ML | 1 OZ. BOURBON
- ★ 15ML | 1/2 OZ. LIME JUICE
- ★ 15 ML | 1/2 OZ. LEMON JUICE
- ★ 1 DASH ANGOSTURA BITTERS
- ★ 150ML | 5 OZ. GINGER BEER
- ★ ICE CUBES

METHOD

1 IN A SHAKER, COMBINE THE BOURBON, GIN, LIME JUICE, LEMON JUICE, AND BITTERS.

2 FILL THE SHAKER WITH ICE CUBES AND SHAKE WELL TO CHILL.

3 STRAIN THE MIXTURE INTO A HIGHBALL GLASS AND FILL WITH ICE.

4 TOP THE GLASS WITH GINGER BEER AND SERVE!

GIBSON

PREP TIME: UNDER 3 MINUTES

IF YOU WANT TO BE THE GUY WITH A DIRTY MARTINI BUT HATE OLIVES, GIVE THIS ONION TWIST A GO.

COMPLEXITY **3** LEVEL

INGREDIENTS

* 75ML | 2 1/2 OZ. GIN (OR VODKA)
* 15ML | 1/2 OZ. DRY VERMOUTH
* COCKTAIL ONION
* ICE CUBES

METHOD

1 FILL A COCKTAIL SHAKER WITH ICE.

2 POUR THE GIN (OR VODKA) AND DRY VERMOUTH INTO THE SHAKER. STIR WELL FOR 20-30 SECONDS TO CHILL THE MIXTURE.

3 STRAIN THE INGREDIENTS INTO A CHILLED MARTINI GLASS.

4 GARNISH WITH 2-3 COCKTAIL ONIONS ON A COCKTAIL SKEWER AND ENJOY!

LONG ISLAND ICED TEA

PREP TIME: UNDER 3 MINUTES

THE RULE IS: THE MORE ALCOHOL YOU DRINK AT ONE TIME, THE MANLIER IT IS.

COMPLEXITY LEVEL 4

INGREDIENTS

* 25ML \ 1 OZ. VODKA
* 25ML \ 1 OZ. WHITE RUM
* 25ML \ 1 OZ. TEQUILA
* 25ML \ 1 OZ. GIN
* 25ML \ 1 OZ. TRIPLE SEC
* 15ML \ 1/2 OZ. SIMPLE SYRUP
* 45ML \ 1 1/2 OZ. LEMON JUICE
* 50ML \ 2 OZ. COLA
* ICE CUBES

METHOD

1 FILL A COCKTAIL SHAKER WITH ICE.

2 ADD THE VODKA, RUM, GIN, TEQUILA, TRIPLE SEC, SIMPLE SYRUP, AND LEMON INTO THE SHAKER.

3 SHAKE THE INGREDIENTS WELL FOR 20 SECONDS TO CHILL THE MIXTURE.

4 FILL A HIGHBALL GLASS WITH ICE AND STRAIN IN THE MIXTURE.

5 TOP WITH YOUR COLA AND GARNISH WITH A SLICE OF LEMON!

MOSCOW MULE

PREP TIME: UNDER 3 MINUTES

CRISP AND REFRESHING WITH A GINGER KICK, THIS IS A GREAT GO-TO WITHOUT LOSING ANY MAN POINTS!

COMPLEXITY LEVEL **2**

INGREDIENTS

* 50ML | 2 OZ. VODKA
* 100ML | 4 OZ. GINGER BEER
* 15ML | 1/2 OZ. LIME JUICE
* LIME WEDGE
* ICE CUBES

METHOD

1 FILL A HIGHBALL GLASS WITH ICE.

2 POUR THE VODKA AND LIME JUICE INTO THE GLASS.

3 TOP WITH GINGER BEER AND STIR GENTLY TO COMBINE.

4 GARNISH WITH A LIME WEDGE.

VESPER MARTINI

PREP TIME: UNDER 3 MINUTES

STEP INTO THE WORLD OF JAMES BOND
WITH 007'S FAVORITE DRINK HIMSELF!

COMPLEXITY
2
LEVEL

INGREDIENTS

- 65ML | 2 1/2 OZ. GIN
- 25ML | 1 OZ. VODKA
- 15ML | 1/2 OZ. LILLET BLANC
  (OR COCCHI AMERICANO)
- LEMON TWIST
- ICE CUBES

METHOD

1 FILL A COCKTAIL SHAKER WITH ICE.

2 POUR THE GIN, VODKA, AND LILLET BLANC INTO THE
SHAKER. SHAKE AND DON'T STIR - OBVIOUSLY!

3 STRAIN INTO A CHILLED MARTINI GLASS.

4 TWIST YOUR LEMON PEEL OVER THE DRINK TO
RELEASE THE OILS, THEN DROP IT INTO THE GLASS.

5 ENJOY WHILST LIVING OUT YOUR SECRET SERVICE
SPY DREAMS!

FOUR HORSEMEN

PREP TIME: UNDER 2 MINUTES

THIS SHOT IS PERFECT FOR WHISKEY LOVERS WHO CAN'T MAKE THEIR MIND UP. JUST HAVE A BIT OF EVERYTHING!

COMPLEXITY LEVEL 1

INGREDIENTS

* ★ 1/4 SHOT BOURBON WHISKEY
* ★ 1/4 SHOT TENNESSEE WHISKEY
* ★ 1/4 SHOT SCOTCH WHISKY
* ★ 1/4 SHOT IRISH WHISKY

METHOD

1 POUR ALL INGREDIENTS INTO A SHOT GLASS AND ENJOY!

OTHER VARIATIONS:

FOUR HORSEMEN IN A BOAT - REPLACE THE IRISH WHISKY WITH GOLD TEQUILA, ADD 1/2 SHOT ORANGE LIQUEUR AND SERVE OVER ICE!

FOUR HORSEMEN MEET A PIRATE - SIMILAR TO THE ABOVE, BUT SWAP THE ORANGE LIQUEUR FOR SPICED RUM.

THREE WISE MEN - ANY THREE OF THE ORIGINAL HORSEMEN, IN A SHOT GLASS.

HOT TODDY

PREP TIME: 10 MINUTES

THE MAN'S ANSWER TO MULLED WINE, THE HOT TODDY IS PERFECT FOR WARMING UP IN THOSE COOLER MONTHS!

COMPLEXITY LEVEL **4**

INGREDIENTS

- ★ 60ML | 2 OZ. WHISKEY
- ★ 1 TBSP. HONEY
- ★ 15ML | 1/2 OZ. LEMON JUICE
- ★ HOT WATER
- ★ LEMON SLICE
- ★ CINNAMON STICK

METHOD

1 IN A HEATPROOF MUG, COMBINE THE WHISKEY, HONEY, AND LEMON.

2 ADD THE WATER AND STIR TO COMBINE.

3 GARNISH WITH A LEMON SLICE AND ALLOW TO INFUSE.

TOP TIP: ADD CLOVES AND STAR ANISE FOR MORE WARMING SPICE.

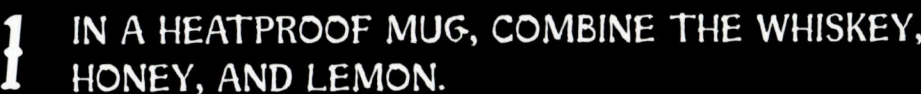

GETTING THE MOST OUT OF YOUR CITRUS

MANY COCKTAILS CALL FOR THE USE OF CITRUS, WHETHER AS A GARNISH OR AN INGREDIENT. HERE ARE A FEW KEY WAYS TO MAKE SURE YOU GET THE MOST OUT OF THIS INGREDIENT.

ALWAYS USE FRESH

THERE IS NO SUBSTITUTE FOR FRESH CITRUS. MAKE SURE YOU ALWAYS USE A FRESH FRUIT RATHER THAN ANY SORT OF BOTTLED JUICE ALTERNATIVE – WHEN IT COMES TO COCKTAILS IT SIMPLY WON'T DO!

ROLL YOUR CITRUS

DOES YOUR RECIPE CALL FOR THE JUICE OF A LEMON OR LIME? PLACE IT ON A HARD SURFACE AND PLACE THE HEEL OF YOUR PALM ON TOP. APPLY SOME PRESSURE, THEN ROLL BACKWARDS AND FORWARDS UNDER YOUR HAND. THIS ENSURES THAT WHEN YOU COME TO SQUEEZING THE FRUIT, YOU GET THE MOST JUICE OUT AS YOU CAN!

WEDGE, WHEEL OR TWIST?

THE DIFFERENCE BETWEEN THESE TYPES OF GARNISHES WILL MASSIVELY CHANGE YOUR COCKTAIL.

WEDGE – WEDGES OF CITRUS ARE GREAT FOR WHEN YOU MIGHT WANT TO ADD A LITTLE EXTRA FLAVOR TO YOUR DRINK. LIME IS THE MOST COMMON WEDGE GARNISH, AND WE'D ALWAYS RECOMMEND GIVING IT A SQUEEZE!

WHEEL – A CITRUS WHEEL IS SIMPLY A CIRCULAR SLICE (OR CROSS-SECTION) OF YOUR CITRUS FRUIT. THEY ADD FRUITY AROMAS FROM THE OILS AND PEELS, AND JUICY FLAVOR FROM THE FLESH. BY ADDING A SLIT FROM THE EDGE TO THE CENTER, YOU CAN ELEGANTLY POSITION YOUR WHEEL ON THE EDGE OF THE GLASS. SQUEEZE YOUR WHEEL FOR AN EXTRA POP OF FLAVOR!

TWIST – THE CITRUS TWIST IS THE MOST CLASSIC AND WIDELY USED COCKTAIL GARNISH. ITS ELEGANT VISUAL APPEAL, AND AROMATIC OILS ADD A LAYER OF NUANCE AND DEPTH TO COCKTAILS.

SNAKEBITE

PREP TIME: UNDER 1 MINUTE

POPULARIZED IN THE UK IN THE 1980S, A SNAKEBITE IS PERFECT IF YOU CAN'T MAKE YOUR MIND UP BETWEEN HARD CIDER AND BEER.

COMPLEXITY LEVEL 1

INGREDIENTS

* 250ML | 8.5 OZ. LAGER BEER
* 250ML | 8.5 OZ. HARD CIDER

METHOD

1 IN A BEER GLASS, POUR YOUR HARD CIDER. SLOWLY ADD YOUR BEER AND ENJOY!

TOP TIP: IN BRITAIN, THEY MIGHT ALSO ADD BLACKCURRANT CORDIAL AND CALL THIS A 'SNAKEBITE AND BLACK', AND IS A GREAT SWEET PINT OF ALCOHOL (ALTHOUGH NOT QUITE AS MANLY AS THE ORIGINAL DEAL).

SIDECAR

PREP TIME: UNDER 3 MINUTES

BALANCED, CLASSIC, AND DEFINITELY BOOZY, THE SIDECAR IS A COCKTAIL THAT CUTS OUT THE FRILLS!

COMPLEXITY LEVEL **2**

INGREDIENTS

* 60ML | 2 OZ. BRANDY
* 30ML | 1 OZ. TRIPLE SEC
* 20ML | 3/4 OZ. LEMON JUICE
* LEMON PEEL TWIST

METHOD

1 FILL A COCKTAIL SHAKER WITH ICE.

2 COMBINE THE BRANDY, TRIPLE SEC, AND LEMON JUICE.

3 SHAKE WELL UNTIL CHILLED.

4 STRAIN INTO A MARTINI GLASS.

5 GARNISH WITH A LEMON PEEL TWIST, AND ENJOY!

MAI TAI

PREP TIME: UNDER 3 MINUTES

ELVIS FAMOUSLY LOVED A MAI TAI. IF IT'S GOOD ENOUGH FOR THE KING OF ROCK AND ROLL, IT'S GOOD ENOUGH FOR YOU.

COMPLEXITY
3
LEVEL

INGREDIENTS

- 50ML \ 2 OZ. DARK RUM
- 25ML \ 1 OZ. WHITE RUM
- 25ML \ 1 OZ. TRIPLE SEC
- 25ML \ 1 OZ. LIME JUICE
- 10ML \ 1/2 OZ. ORGEAT (ALMOND SYRUP)
- 10ML \ 1/2 OZ. SIMPLE SYRUP
- CRUSHED ICE

METHOD

1 FILL A SHAKER WITH CRUSHED ICE.

2 ADD THE DARK RUM, WHITE RUM, TRIPLE SEC, LIME JUICE, ORGEAT SYRUP, AND SIMPLE SYRUP TO THE SHAKER.

3 SHAKE THE INGREDIENTS WELL FOR 20 SECONDS TO CHILL.

4 STRAIN THE MIXTURE INTO A ROCKS GLASS AND FILL WITH CRUSHED ICE.

WHISKEY AND WATER

PREP TIME: UNDER 1 MINUTE

MORE THAN ONE INGREDIENT? THIS DEFINITELY COUNTS AS A COCKTAIL. THE AMOUNT OF WATER YOU USE COULD DETERMINE JUST HOW MANLY IT IS...

COMPLEXITY LEVEL 1

INGREDIENTS

- ★ WHISKEY
- ★ WATER

METHOD

1 ADDING WATER TO WHISKEY ALLOWS YOU TO TASTE THE WHISKEY FLAVOR MORE, WITHOUT BEING TOO DISTRACTED BY THE ALCOHOL BURN. THE AMOUNT VARIES DEPENDING ON YOUR TASTES.

2 START BY ADDING 4-5 DROPS TO YOUR NEAT WHISKEY. CONTINUE UNTIL THE WHISKEY IS DRINKABLE ENOUGH FOR YOU!

GIN AND TONIC

PREP TIME: UNDER 5 MINUTES

LEAVE THE LEMON AT HOME. JUNIPER BERRIES? WHAT EVEN ARE THEY? WITHOUT THE FRILLS, YOU CAN HAVE A GIN AND TONIC AND STILL LOOK LIKE THE REAL MAN YOU ARE.

COMPLEXITY LEVEL 2

INGREDIENTS

* 50ML | 2 OZ. GIN
* 100ML | 4 OZ. TONIC WATER
* CUCUMBER SLICES FOR GARNISH
* ICE CUBES

METHOD

1 FILL A ROCKS GLASS WITH ICE.

2 POUR OVER YOUR CHOSEN GIN - HENDRICK'S IS A CLASSIC CHOICE.

3 FILL WITH TONIC TO YOUR DESIRED PREFERENCE.

4 ADD SOME THINLY SLICED CUCUMBER AND SERVE!

MOJITO

PREP TIME: UNDER 3 MINUTES

A MOJITO MIGHT SEEM LIKE IT ISN'T VERY MANLY, YOU KNOW - WITH ALL THE LEAVES AND STUFF. HOWEVER, NO ONE CAN ARGUE WITH THIS CUBAN DELICACY.

COMPLEXITY LEVEL 3

INGREDIENTS

* ★ 60ML | 2 OZ. WHITE RUM
* ★ 1/2 LIME (CUT INTO WEDGES)
* ★ 2 TSP. GRANULATED SUGAR
* ★ 6-8 FRESH MINT LEAVES
* ★ 120ML | 4 OZ. SODA WATER
* ★ ICE CUBES

METHOD

1 IN A HIGHBALL GLASS, MUDDLE YOUR LIME AND SUGAR UNTIL THE SUGAR DISSOLVES AND THE LIME IS JUICED.

2 ADD THE MINT LEAVES AND MUDDLE GENTLY TO RELEASE THEIR OILS.

3 FILL THE GLASS WITH ICE, ADD YOUR RUM AND TOP WITH SODA WATER.

4 STIR THE MIXTURE GENTLY.

5 SERVE WITH A LIME SLICE AND MINT SPRIG - ENJOY!

BLOODY BULL

PREP TIME: 5 MINUTES

EVER THOUGHT THAT YOUR DRINK WAS MISSING A BIT OF BEEF? TIME TO LIVE THE DREAM WITH THE BLOODY BULL - A MEATY TWIST ON THE BLOODY MARY!

COMPLEXITY
3
LEVEL

INGREDIENTS

- ★ 45ML \ 1 1/2 OZ. VODKA
- ★ 120ML \ 4 OZ. TOMATO JUICE
- ★ 30ML \ 1 OZ. BEEF BROTH
- ★ 15ML \ 1/2 OZ. LEMON JUICE
- ★ 1/2 TSP. HORSERADISH
- ★ 1/2 TSP. HOT SAUCE
- ★ 1/2 TSP. WORCESTERSHIRE SAUCE
- ★ CELERY FOR GARNISH
- ★ SALT AND PEPPER TO TASTE

METHOD

1 IN A MIXING GLASS, COMBINE ALL INGREDIENTS. STIR WELL.

2 ADD ICE AND SLOWLY STIR UNTIL CHILLED. TRANSFER TO A GLASS.

3 GARNISH WITH YOUR CELERY STICK AND ENJOY.

TOP TIP: ADD AS MUCH BEEF BROTH AS YOUR HEART DESIRES!

GOLD RUSH

PREP TIME: UNDER 3 MINUTES

BOLD AND BALANCED, THE GOLD RUSH IS SURE TO LEAVE A LASTING IMPRESSION.

COMPLEXITY

2

LEVEL

INGREDIENTS

* 60ML | 2 OZ. BOURBON
* 20ML | 3/4 OZ. LEMON JUICE
* 15ML | 1/2 OZ. HONEY
* 15ML | 1/2 OZ. WATER

METHOD

1 FILL A COCKTAIL SHAKER WITH ICE.

2 ADD THE BOURBON, LEMON JUICE, HONEY, AND WATER TO THE SHAKER.

3 SHAKE WELL FOR 15-20 SECONDS, UNTIL COLD.

4 FILL A ROCKS GLASS WITH ICE. POUR THE MIXTURE OVER THE ICE AND SERVE!

SHAKEN OR STIRRED?

WE ALL KNOW JAMES BOND IS VERY PARTICULAR ABOUT THE WAY HIS MARTINI IS PREPARED... BUT HIS METHOD BRINGS DESPAIR TO BARTENDERS ALL ACROSS THE GLOBE.

THERE'S REASONS WHY MARTINIS ARE STIRRED AND NOT SHAKEN!

AS WITH EVERY COCKTAIL. THE WAY YOUR DRINK IS PREPARED CAN MASSIVELY AFFECT THE FLAVOR AND TEXTURE.

SHAKING A COCKTAIL WITH ICE DILUTES IT, AS THE FRICTION BETWEEN THE ICE AND THE LIQUID FROM SHAKING GENERATES HEAT, MELTING THE ICE. SHAKING IS ALSO USED TO CHANGE THE TEXTURE OF THE DRINK, AS THE SHAKING PROCESS AERATES THE LIQUID – THINK ABOUT THE FOAMY TOP OF AN ESPRESSO MARTINI.

STIRRING A COCKTAIL WITH ICE MERELY CHILLS THE DRINK, AND DOES NOT DILUTE IT NEARLY AS MUCH AS SHAKING DOES. IN FACT, OTHER THAN A FEW NOTABLE EXCEPTIONS SUCH AS THE OLD FASHIONED, DRINKS ARE NEVER STIRRED FOR MORE THAN 30 TO 45 SECONDS.

TO DIRECTLY COMPARE- SHAKING A DRINK FOR 15 TO 20 SECONDS CAN ACHIEVE THE SAME DEGREE OF COOLING AND DILUTION AS STIRRING A DRINK FOR 90 TO 120 SECONDS.

SO WHEN JAMES BOND DEMANDS HIS MARTINI TO BE SHAKEN, NOT STIRRED, THE STRONG FLAVORS ARE ALTERED AND HIS DRINK IS DILUTED.

MAYBE HE'S NOT AS MANLY AS HE MAKES OUT!

CUBA LIBRE

PREP TIME: UNDER 3 MINUTES

AN ELEVATED RUM AND COKE, THE CUBA LIBRE WILL HAVE EVEN THE SIMPLEST OF MEN SOUNDING SOPHISTICATED.

COMPLEXITY 2 LEVEL

INGREDIENTS

* 60ML | 2 OZ. WHITE RUM
* 15ML | 1/2 OZ. LIME JUICE
* 120ML | 4 OZ. COLA
* LIME WEDGE
* ICE CUBES

METHOD

1 FILL A HIGHBALL GLASS WITH ICE CUBES.

2 POUR THE RUM INTO THE GLASS.

3 ADD THE LIME JUICE OVER THE RUM.

4 FILL WITH COLA AND STIR GENTLY.

5 GARNISH WITH A LIME WEDGE AND ENJOY!

FIERY GERMAN

PREP TIME: UNDER 2 MINUTES

THIS SPICY AND HERBAL SHORT DRINK IS NOT FOR THE FAINT OF HEART - BUT FOR THE JÄGERMEISTER FANS OUT THERE... THIS COULD BE YOUR NEW FAVORITE.

COMPLEXITY LEVEL 1

INGREDIENTS

- ★ 30ML \ 1 OZ. JÄGERMEISTER
- ★ 30ML \ 1 OZ. CINNAMON SCHNAPPS
- ★ ICE CUBES

METHOD

1 FILL A COCKTAIL SHAKER WITH ICE.

2 POUR THE JÄGERMEISTER AND SCHNAPPS INTO THE SHAKER AND SHAKE THOROUGHLY FOR 15 SECONDS.

3 STRAIN INTO A CHILLED ROCKS GLASS AND ENJOY!

HORSEFEATHER

PREP TIME: UNDER 3 MINUTES

A WHISKEY TWIST ON THE CLASSIC MOSCOW MULE, SOME MAY EVEN CONSIDER THIS COCKTAIL THE MANLIER VERSION.

COMPLEXITY LEVEL 2

INGREDIENTS

- ICE
- 60ML | 2 OZ. WHISKEY
- 120ML | 4 OZ. GINGER BEER
- 4 DASHES ANGOSTURA BITTERS
- LEMON OR LIME WEDGE

METHOD

1 FILL A HIGHBALL GLASS WITH ICE.

2 ADD WHISKEY, GINGER BEER, BITTERS, AND A SQUEEZE OF CITRUS, THEN STIR TO COMBINE.

3 GARNISH WITH EXTRA LEMON OR LIME AND ENJOY.

GREYHOUND

PREP TIME: UNDER 3 MINUTES

SIMPLE WITH A HINT OF FRUITINESS, YOU GET EXTRA MAN POINTS IF YOU DON'T PULL A FACE WHILST DRINKING THIS SOUR DRINK!

COMPLEXITY LEVEL 2

INGREDIENTS

* 90 ML | 3 OZ. GRAPEFRUIT JUICE
* 45ML | 1 ½ OZ. VODKA
* ICE
* LEMON OR LIME WEDGE

METHOD

1 ADD ICE, GRAPEFRUIT, AND VODKA TO A COCKTAIL SHAKER. SHAKE TO CHILL.

2 STRAIN INTO A ROCKS GLASS OVER ICE.

3 GARNISH WITH CITRUS WEDGE OF CHOICE.

TOP TIP: ADD A SALT RIM TO THIS DRINK AND YOU HAVE YOURSELF A 'SALTY DOG.'

WHISKEY SMASH

PREP TIME: UNDER 3 MINUTES

WHEN YOU THINK WHISKEY, YOU MAY NOT IMMEDIATELY THINK MINT. BUT TRUST US WHEN WE SAY, THESE TWO GO TOGETHER LIKE A HOUSE ON FIRE.

COMPLEXITY LEVEL 4

INGREDIENTS

- ★ 8 MINT LEAVES
- ★ 2 LEMON SLICES
- ★ 1 SUGAR
- ★ 60ML | 2 OZ. WHISKEY
- ★ CRUSHED ICE
- ★ MINT SPRIG AND POWDERED SUGAR FOR GARNISH

METHOD

1 IN A COCKTAIL SHAKER, MUDDLE MINT LEAVES WITH LEMON AND SUGAR.

2 ADD ICE AND WHISKEY, THEN SHAKE TO CHILL.

3 STRAIN INTO A ROCKS GLASS OVER FRESH ICE.

4 GARNISH WITH A MINT SPRIG AND A DUSTING OF POWDERED SUGAR.

TOP TIP: POWDERED SUGAR NOT MANLY ENOUGH? YOU CAN LEAVE IT OUT.

PENICILLIN

PREP TIME: UNDER 3 MINUTES

PENICILLIN IS ONE OF THE GREATEST DISCOVERIES IN HUMAN HISTORY. SECOND ONLY TO THE DISCOVERY OF THIS DRINK. SMOKY, SPICY, AND SOUR – SOMEONE CALL A DOCTOR!

COMPLEXITY
2
LEVEL

INGREDIENTS

* 25ML | ¾ OZ. FRESHLY SQUEEZED LEMON JUICE
* 25ML | ¾ OZ. GINGER-INFUSED SIMPLE SYRUP
* 60ML | 2 OZ. BLENDED SCOTCH
* 30ML | ½ OZ. ISLAY SCOTCH
* ICE

METHOD

1 IN A COCKTAIL SHAKER, ADD ALL INGREDIENTS.

2 SHAKE UNTIL CHILLED.

3 STRAIN INTO A ROCKS GLASS OVER FRESH ICE, AND DRINK IMMEDIATELY.

STINGER

PREP TIME: UNDER 3 MINUTES

HERE'S A COCKTAIL THAT FLOATS LIKE A BUTTERFLY AND STINGS LIKE A BEE. THE STRONG, BOOZY MINT FLAVOR WILL DEFINITELY WAKE YOU UP - LIKE A PUNCH TO THE FACE!

COMPLEXITY LEVEL 2

INGREDIENTS

- 30ML \ 1 OZ. WHITE CRÈME DE MENTHE
- 60ML \ 2 OZ. COGNAC
- ICE
- MINT SPRIG AND LEMON WHEEL FOR GARNISH

METHOD

1 IN A MIXING GLASS, ADD ICE, WHITE CRÈME DE MENTHE, AND COGNAC.

2 STIR RAPIDLY TO CHILL.

3 STRAIN INTO A ROCKS GLASS OVER FRESH ICE.

4 GARNISH WITH MINT SPRIG AND LEMON WHEEL, AND ENJOY!

WHITE RUSSIAN

PREP TIME: UNDER 2 MINUTES

WHILE SOME MAY NOT CONSIDER WHITE RUSSIANS A MANLY DRINK, WE REMIND THEM THAT THEY ARE MANLY IF THE ALTERNATIVE IS A MILKSHAKE!

COMPLEXITY 2 LEVEL

INGREDIENTS

* 60ML | 2 OZ. VODKA
* 30ML | 1 OZ. KAHLÚA
* 30ML | 1 OZ. HEAVY CREAM

METHOD

1 ADD THE VODKA AND KAHLÚA TO A ROCKS GLASS FILLED WITH ICE.

2 TOP WITH HEAVY CREAM AND STIR.

TOP TIP: USE LARGE BITS OF ICE FOR THIS DRINK AND AVOID SMALL SHARDS, AS THESE WILL MELT QUICKLY AND DILUTE YOUR CREAMY DRINK!

THE ANATOMY OF A COCKTAIL SHAKER

GET TO KNOW A BARTENDER'S BEST FRIEND!

WHICH SHAKER?

THE COBBLER SHAKER (OR 3-PIECE COCKTAIL SHAKER) INCLUDES A SHAKER TIN, LID WITH BUILT IN STRAINER, AND A CAP TO KEEP THINGS CLOSED WHILST YOU SHAKE. THIS IS A GREAT BEGINNER'S CHOICE, AND IS MOST LIKELY TO BE THE COCKTAIL SHAKER YOU HAVE AT HOME. THE BOSTON SHAKER IS THE PROFESSIONAL BARTENDER'S GO-TO SHAKER. IT HAS TWO PARTS: A LARGE SHAKER TIN AND A SMALLER SHAKER TIN. WITH THIS SHAKER YOU NEED A SEPARATE COCKTAIL STRAINER, AND BEGINNERS MAY FIND IT TRICKY TO USE AT FIRST, AS THERE'S A KNACK TO SECURING AND SEPARATING IT.

SHAKING YOUR COCKTAIL

YOUR INSTINCT IS PROBABLY TO SHAKE THE SHAKER IN AN UP AND DOWN MOTION, BUT THIS ISN'T THE MOST EFFECTIVE METHOD. INSTEAD, A HORIZONTAL MOTION (THAT DOESN'T WORK AGAINST GRAVITY) WILL GIVE YOU A MOST EFFECTIVE SHAKE. HOW TO MASTER IT? HOLD YOUR SHAKER ABOVE YOUR SHOULDER AND BY YOUR HEAD ON ONE SIDE. BRING THE SHAKER FORWARDS AND BACKWARDS. USE THE MOTION OF THE LIQUID INSIDE TO POWER YOUR SHAKE, AND REMEMBER TO SHAKE AS HARD AS YOU CAN – THE QUICKER AND HARDER THE BETTER!

SAZERAC

PREP TIME: UNDER 5 MINUTES

FEATURING AN ABSINTHE RINSE, THIS COCKTAIL IS NOT FOR THE FAINT OF HEART (OR MEN WHO HATE LICORICE).

COMPLEXITY
2
LEVEL

INGREDIENTS

- ★ ABSINTHE (TO RINSE)
- ★ 1 SUGAR CUBE
- ★ ½ TEASPOON COLD WATER
- ★ 4 DASHES PEYCHAUD'S BITTERS
- ★ 75ML | 2 ½ OZ. RYE WHISKEY
- ★ LEMON PEEL

METHOD

1 POUR A SPLASH OR SO OF ABSINTHE INTO A ROCKS GLASS AND SWIRL, COVERING THE SURFACES OF THE GLASS, THEN DISCARD ANY EXCESS.

2 MUDDLE THE SUGAR CUBE, WATER, AND PEYCHAUD'S BITTERS IN A MIXING GLASS.

3 ADD THE RYE WHISKEY, FILL THE MIXING GLASS WITH ICE, AND STIR FOR 15-20 SECONDS UNTIL WELL-CHILLED.

4 STRAIN INTO THE ROCK GLASS AND TWIST THE LEMON PEEL OVER THE DRINK'S SURFACE TO EXPRESS THE OILS, THEN GARNISH ON THE EDGE OF THE GLASS.

TOP TIP: DON'T WANT TO WASTE YOUR ABSINTHE? THE MANLIEST MEN CAN POUR THE EXCESS INTO A SHOT GLASS TO ENJOY AS A CHASER.

NAVY GROG

PREP TIME: UNDER 3 MINUTES

POTENT AND COMPLEX, THIS CLASSIC TIKI COCKTAIL PACKS A MANLY PUNCH.

COMPLEXITY LEVEL 3

INGREDIENTS

- ★ 30ML \ 1OZ. LIGHT RUM
- ★ 30ML \ 1OZ. JAMAICAN RUM
- ★ 30ML \ 1OZ. DEMERARA RUM
- ★ 30ML \ 1OZ. SIMPLE SUGAR SYRUP
- ★ 20ML \ 3/4 OZ. LIME JUICE
- ★ 20ML \ 3/4 OZ. GRAPEFRUIT JUICE
- ★ LIME AND MINT TO GARNISH

METHOD

1 ADD ALL INGREDIENTS TO A COCKTAIL SHAKER AND FILL WITH ICE.

2 SHAKE UNTIL CHILLED.

3 STRAIN INTO A ROCKS GLASS FILLED WITH ICE.

4 GARNISH WITH A LIME WEDGE AND MINT, AND ENJOY!

CORPSE REVIVER

№ .2

PREP TIME: UNDER 3 MINUTES

THE MORE POPULAR VERSION OF THE CORPSE REVIVER DRINKS, THE ABSINTHE AROMA OF THIS DRINK COULD BRING BACK THE DEAD.

COMPLEXITY **3** LEVEL

INGREDIENTS

- ★ ABSINTHE (TO RINSE)
- ★ 23ML | ¾ OZ. LONDON DRY GIN
- ★ 23ML | ¾ OZ. LILLET BLANC
- ★ 23ML | ¾ OZ. ORANGE LIQUEUR
- ★ 23ML | ¾ OZ. LEMON JUICE, FRESHLY SQUEEZED

METHOD

1 POUR A SPLASH OR SO OF ABSINTHE INTO A CHILLED MARTINI GLASS AND SWIRL, COVERING THE SURFACES OF THE GLASS, THEN DISCARD ANY EXCESS.

2 ADD ALL THE INGREDIENTS INTO A COCKTAIL SHAKER WITH ICE, AND SHAKE UNTIL WELL CHILLED.

3 STRAIN INTO THE MARTINI GLASS, AND DRINK WHILST COLD.

MANHATTAN

PREP TIME: UNDER 3 MINUTES

SMOKY AND COMPLEX, THIS CLASSIC COCKTAIL IS A GREAT GO-TO FOR WHISKEY LOVERS.

COMPLEXITY

3

LEVEL

INGREDIENTS

- 60ML | 2 OZ. WHISKEY
- 30ML | 1 OZ. SWEET VERMOUTH
- 2 DASHES ANGOSTURA BITTERS
- ORANGE PEEL TWIST
- ICE CUBES

METHOD

1 ADD THE WHISKEY, SWEET VERMOUTH, BITTERS, AND ICE INTO A COCKTAIL SHAKER.

2 STIR GENTLY TO CHILL THE DRINK.

3 STRAIN INTO A MARTINI GLASS.

4 TWIST YOUR ORANGE PEEL OVER THE DRINK TO RELEASE THE OILS, THEN DROP IT INTO THE GLASS.

TOM COLLINS

PREP TIME: UNDER 5 MINUTES

THIS CLASSIC BRITISH CONCOCTION WILL HAVE YOU RAISING YOUR PINKY FINGER (IN A MANLY WAY)

COMPLEXITY
1
LEVEL

INGREDIENTS

* 50ML | 2 OZ. GIN
* 25ML | 1/2 OZ. LEMON JUICE
* 25ML | 1/2 OZ. SIMPLE SYRUP
* 90ML | 3 OZ. SODA WATER
* ICE CUBES
* LEMON SLICE

METHOD

1 IN A SHAKER, COMBINE THE GIN, LEMON JUICE, AND SIMPLE SYRUP.

2 FILL THE SHAKER WITH ICE AND SHAKE WELL FOR 20 SECONDS, OR UNTIL THE MIXTURE IS CHILLED.

3 FILL A HIGHBALL GLASS WITH ICE.

4 STRAIN THE MIXTURE INTO THE GLASS, AND TOP WITH SODA WATER.

5 STIR GENTLY TO COMBINE AND SERVE WITH A LEMON SLICE.

MICHELADA

PREP TIME: UNDER 5 MINUTES

AN ELEVATED MARGARITA HAILING FROM MEXICO, THIS DRINK IS SPICY, FLAVORFUL, AND INVOLVES BEER!

COMPLEXITY **4** LEVEL

INGREDIENTS

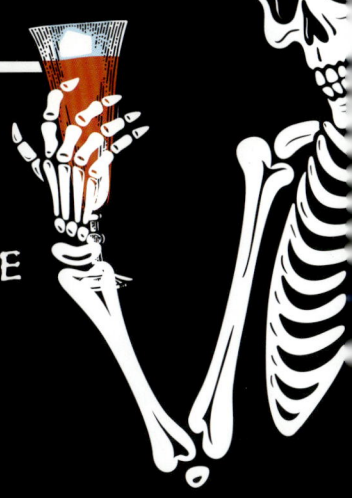

- ★ 300ML \ 12 OZ. LAGER BEER
- ★ 60ML \ 2 OZ. TOMATO JUICE
- ★ 15ML \ 1/2 OZ. LIME JUICE
- ★ 5ML \ 1 TSP. WORCESTERSHIRE SAUCE
- ★ 2.5ML \ 1/2 TSP. HOT SAUCE
- ★ PINCH SALT AND PEPPER
- ★ LIME WEDGE
- ★ ICE CUBES

METHOD

1 RUB A LIME SLICE AROUND THE RIM OF YOUR GLASS, AND RUB THE RIM IN FLAKY SEA SALT AND CHILI POWDER TO CREATE A SALT RIM.

2 FILL THE HIGHBALL GLASS WITH ICE.

3 ADD THE TOMATO JUICE, LIME JUICE, WORCESTERSHIRE SAUCE, HOT SAUCE, SALT AND PEPPER TO THE GLASS.

4 STIR THE INGREDIENTS TOGETHER UNTIL WELL MIXED.

5 POUR THE BEER INTO THE GLASS, STIRRING GENTLY TO COMBINE.

6 SERVE WITH A LIME WEDGE AND ENJOY!

IRISH CAR BOMB

PREP TIME: 2 MINUTES

BOLD AND JUST AS EXPLOSIVE AS THE NAME SUGGESTS, THIS COMBINATION IS ABOUT AS IRISH AS THEY COME!

COMPLEXITY
2
LEVEL

INGREDIENTS

* 15ML \ 1/2 OZ. IRISH WHISKEY
* 15ML \ 1/2 OZ. IRISH CREAM LIQUEUR
* 1 PINT IRISH STOUT BEER (E.G. GUINNESS)

METHOD

1 POUR THE IRISH WHISKEY AND IRISH CREAM LIQUEUR INTO A SHOT GLASS.

2 FILL A PINT GLASS HALFWAY WITH THE IRISH STOUT.

3 DROP THE SHOT GLASS INTO THE STOUT AND IMMEDIATELY DRINK THE CONCOCTION BEFORE IT CURDLES!

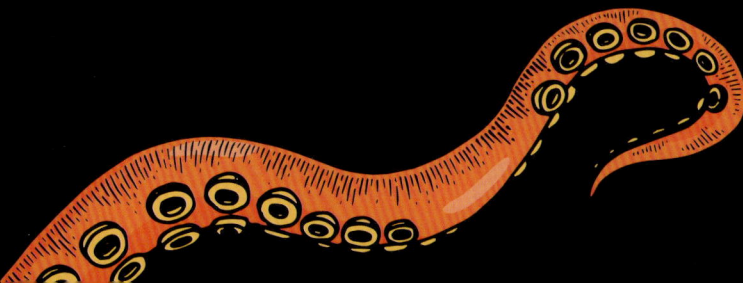

JERSEY TURNPIKE

PREP TIME: AS FAST AS THE BARTENDER IS

THINK YOU MIGHT BE THE MANLIEST MAN? GET YOURSELF A JERSEY TURNPIKE AND GLORY IN THE IMPRESSED (AND DISGUSTED) FACES AROUND YOU.

COMPLEXITY 1 LEVEL

INGREDIENTS

* YOUR GUESS IS AS GOOD AS OURS

METHOD

IF THE BARTENDER DOESN'T KNOW WHAT YOU MEAN WHEN YOU ASK FOR A JERSEY TURNPIKE, JUST GIVE THEM THESE SIMPLE INSTRUCTIONS:

1 POUR ALL THE SPILLED (MYSTERY) LIQUIDS FROM THE BAR MAT INTO A SHOT GLASS.

2 NOT FILLED ALL THE WAY TO THE TOP? NO PROBLEM, JUST WIPE DOWN THE BAR WITH A RAG, THEN SQUEEZE THE LIQUID IN.

THEN YOU JUST... ENJOY?

GREAT GARNISHES

ONE OF THE MOST ICONIC ELEMENTS OF A COCKTAIL ISN'T EVEN PART OF THE COCKTAIL ITSELF – IT'S THE GARNISH.

WE'VE ALREADY COVERED CITRUS GARNISHES EARLIER IN THE BOOK - SO LOOK AT THAT PAGE FOR TIPS ON ALL THINGS LEMON AND LIME. HERE ARE SOME OF THE OTHER MOST POPULAR, AND IMPORTANT, GARNISHES.

HERBS

HERBS - SUCH AS MINT SPRIGS, BASIL LEAVES, OR ROSEMARY STEMS. THESE SUBTLY INFUSE DRINKS WITH THEIR SCENTS AND FLAVORS, AND COMPLEMENT OR CONTRAST THE PRIMARY FLAVORS OF YOUR COCKTAIL. WHEN USING HERBS SUCH AS MINT, TRY GENTLY SLAPPING THEM ON THE BACK OF YOUR HAND TO RELEASE THEIR OILS AND INCREASE THEIR AROMA.

BERRIES AND FRUITS

THESE CAN BE PLACED ON TOP OF YOUR DRINK, SKEWERED OR PLACED ON THE EDGE. THIS ADDS COLOR, TEXTURE, AND TASTE TO YOUR COCKTAIL - AND MAKE A TASTY ALCOHOL INFUSED SNACK.

RIMS

A SALTED, SUGARED, OR FRUIT RIM CHANGES THE FLAVOR AND TEXTURE OF YOUR DRINK WITH EACH SIP. NEXT TIME YOU EXPRESS THE OIL FROM A CITRUS TWIST, TRY RUBBING THE OILS ON THE RIM FOR A STRONGER FLAVOR. FOR AN EVEN SALT AND SUGAR RIM, USE A CITRUS WEDGE TO WET THE GLASS'S EDGE, THEN DIP IN YOUR GARNISH OF CHOICE!

ESPRESSO MARTINI

PREP TIME: UNDER 3 MINUTES

DANGEROUSLY DRINKABLE - THE ESPRESSO MARTINI HAS A KICK OF CAFFEINE, AND ITS SWEETNESS CAN BE TAILORED TO YOUR MANLY TASTE.

COMPLEXITY 3 LEVEL

INGREDIENTS

- 60ML | 2 OZ. VODKA
- 30ML | 1 OZ. COFFEE LIQUEUR (SUCH AS KAHLUA)
- 30ML | 1 OZ. ROOM TEMPERATURE COFFEE ESPRESSO
- 1 TBSP. SIMPLE SUGAR SYRUP (OR TO TASTE)
- ICE

METHOD

1 POUR ALL INGREDIENTS INTO THE COCKTAIL SHAKER AND ADD ICE.

2 SHAKE HARD, UNTIL THE OUTSIDE IS COLD.

3 STRAIN INTO A CHILLED MARTINI GLASS.

4 GARNISH WITH COFFEE BEANS IF AVAILABLE!

TRADITIONAL ABSINTHE

PREP TIME: UNDER 5 MINUTES

IF THERE'S ONE COCKTAIL THAT WILL DIVIDE OPINIONS, IT'S THIS ONE. SURE TO PUT SOME HAIRS ON YOUR CHEST, THIS MAY BE AS MANLY AS COCKTAILS GET.

COMPLEXITY
2
LEVEL

INGREDIENTS

* 60ML | 2 OZ. ABSINTHE
* 180ML | 6 OZ. COLD WATER
* 1-2 SUGAR CUBES
* A SLOTTED SPOON

METHOD

1 POUR THE ABSINTHE INTO A ROCKS GLASS.

2 BALANCE THE SPOON ACROSS THE GLASS AND PLACE THE CUBES ON THE SPOONS HEAD.

3 SLOWLY POUR THE WATER OVER THE SUGAR AND SPOON.

4 REMOVE THE SPOON AND ENJOY – VERY, VERY SLOWLY.

THE PALOMA

PREP TIME: UNDER 2 MINUTES

THE NATIONAL DRINK OF MEXICO, DON'T BE FOOLED BY THIS DRINK'S SLIGHT PINK TINGE. THE SOUR NOTES MAKE THIS A MANLY ALTERNATIVE TO THE CLASSIC MARGARITA.

COMPLEXITY
2
LEVEL

INGREDIENTS

- 60ML | 2 OZ. TEQUILA
- 15ML | ½ OZ. LIME JUICE, FRESHLY SQUEEZED
- 120ML | 4 OZ. GRAPEFRUIT SODA
- PINCH OF SALT
- LIME WHEEL TO GARNISH

METHOD

1 ADD THE TEQUILA, LIME JUICE, AND PINCH OF SALT TO A HIGHBALL GLASS, AND FILL WITH ICE.

2 TOP WITH THE GRAPEFRUIT SODA, AND STIR GENTLY TO COMBINE THE INGREDIENTS.

3 GARNISH WITH A LIME WHEEL, AND ENJOY!

ROB ROY

PREP TIME: 3 MINUTES

A SCOTTISH TWIST ON THE MANHATTAN, THIS DRINK'S NAMESAKE WAS A SCOTTISH OUTLAW AND FOLK HERO, AND, WE HEAR, VERY MANLY.

COMPLEXITY LEVEL 1

INGREDIENTS

* 60ML | 2 OZ. SCOTCH WHISKY
* 23ML | ¾ OZ. SWEET VERMOUTH
* 3 DASHES ANGOSTURA BITTERS

METHOD

1 ADD THE SCOTCH, SWEET VERMOUTH, AND BITTERS INTO A MIXING GLASS WITH ICE CUBES AND STIR SLOWLY AND GENTLY UNTIL CHILLED.

2 STRAIN INTO A GLASS AND ENJOY – YOU'LL WANT TO SAVOR THIS ONE.

EL PRESIDENTE

PREP TIME: UNDER 3 MINUTES

HAILED AS 'THE ARISTOCRAT OF COCKTAILS', EL PRESIDENTE IS A CLASSIC CUBAN COCKTAIL, WHICH IS SWEET AND FRUITY BUT LOOKS AS MANLY AS AN OLD FASHIONED.

COMPLEXITY
1
LEVEL

INGREDIENTS

* 45ML | 1 ½ OZ. WHITE RUM
* 15ML | ¾ OZ. DRY VERMOUTH
* 7ML | ¼ OZ. ORANGE LIQUEUR
* 2 DASHES GRENADINE

METHOD

1 ADD ALL THE INGREDIENTS INTO A MIXING GLASS WITH ICE AND STIR UNTIL CHILLED.

2 STRAIN INTO A CHILLED MARTINI GLASS AND ENJOY!

THE SIMPLE SUGAR SYRUP

SUGAR SYRUP IS A CENTRAL INGREDIENT TO MANY COCKTAILS, ADDING A TOUCH OF SWEETNESS THAT COMPLEMENTS CITRUSY OR SMOKY FLAVORS. YOU CAN BUY IT, BUT IT'S ALSO EASY TO MAKE AT HOME, AND CAN KEEP FOR UP TO A MONTH.

INGREDIENTS

* 100G | ½ CUP GRANULATED SUGAR
* 120ML | ½ CUP WATER

METHOD

1 ADD THE SUGAR AND WATER TO A SMALL SAUCEPAN OVER A MEDIUM HEAT.

2 GENTLY STIR UNTIL ALL THE SUGAR IS DISSOLVED.

3 ALLOW TO COOL, THEN POUR INTO A GLASS JAR AND SEAL TIGHTLY.

TO ELEVATE YOUR SIMPLE SUGAR SYRUP, TRY ADDING DIFFERENT ELEMENTS! INFUSE WITH MINT OR ROSEMARY FOR AN HERBACEOUS SYRUP, ADD JALAPEÑOS FOR A FIERY KICK, OR ADD A FEW DROPS OF VANILLA FOR A SWEET AND AROMATIC FLAVOR.

DUCK FART

PREP TIME: UNDER 2 MINUTES

POTENT BUT SWEET, THIS SHOT SLIDES DOWN THE GULLET LIKE WATER OFF A DUCK'S... FART?

COMPLEXITY LEVEL 1

INGREDIENTS

- ★ 1/2 OZ. KAHLÚA
- ★ 1/2 OZ. BAILEY'S IRISH CREAM
- ★ 1/2 OZ. WHISKEY

METHOD

1 START WITH THE KAHLUA FOR THE BOTTOM LAYER.

2 SLOWLY ADD IN THE BAILEY'S, POURING OVER THE BACK OF A SPOON.

3 ADD THE WHISKEY FOR THE TOP LAYER, USING THE SAME TECHNIQUE.

BRAIN HEMMORRHAGE

PREP TIME: UNDER 2 MINUTES

NAMED FOR ITS CREEPY APPEARANCE (AND THANKFULLY NOT ITS EFFECT ON YOUR BRAIN), THIS IS THE ULTIMATE HALLOWEEN SHOT.

COMPLEXITY
2
LEVEL

INGREDIENTS

* 1 OZ. CHILLED PEACH SCHNAPPS
* 1 TSP. CHILLED IRISH CREAM LIQUEUR (SUCH AS BAILEY'S)
* 1 SPLASH CHILLED GRENADINE SYRUP

METHOD

1. POUR SCHNAPPS INTO A SHOT GLASS.

2. GENTLY POUR BAILEY'S ON TOP; LET SIT UNTIL IT BEGINS TO CLUMP AND CURDLE.

3. GENTLY POUR IN GRENADINE.